ARNOLD ADOFF

SLOW DANCE HEART BREAK BLUES

WITH ARTWORK BY WILLIAM COTTON

Lothrop, Lee & Shepard Books
New York

First Edition   3 4 5 6 7 8 9 10
Library of Congress Cataloging in Publication Data
Adoff, Arnold. Slow dance heart break blues /
by Arnold Adoff; illustrated by William Cotton.
p.   cm.
ISBN 0-688-10569-6 1. Love poetry, American.
2. Young adult poetry, American.
[1. Love—Poetry. 2. American poetry.]
I. Cotton, William, 1965-
ill. II. Title. PS3551.D66S56 1995
811'.54—dc20 94-48242 CIP AC

Dedication:

You	Know	I	Love
You	All		
But	This	One Is	
		For Me	

slow dance heart break blues:

falling

in the hall   falling   falling falling up against the wall
after the fall   legs like twisted rubberpretzels   cartoon
birdies spinning around my head   as   she   walks   by a n d
stares   down   at   the   soles   of   my   simple   simon shoes
needing

to learn to dance   dance with mom   dance with dad
dance alone to the   zeppelence   building a s t a i r   way
to   prince and blonde rinse   in some celestial b a llroom
listening

to   the   music   dance   to   the   music   o   sly one
what does she listen to   what does she dance to   who her
favorite singers   favorite bands   favorite styles of long
hair long stare   world class big shirt   kente cloth   funk
bumping

into her in the street   and how many   times a day
is she after school   walking with friends into local   pop
shop burger joints   with her face   fast forward past mine
meeting

the sight of her disappearing back   down the mice
maze of mall halls seeing her later at   sat mat   cinemas
walking the narrow   miles of aisles   of   on sale   ceedees
my   head   full   of   puns   and   roses   until   closing time
finally
attacking

in the middle of the middle of the night   the zit
monsters find the face fast beyond midnight   beyond that
small light seeping under the bathroom door   they   reach
the   very   center   the nose tip h e i g h t   that highest
geographic elevation featured on that face   this face the
forward position of my forward moving daily self   my face
will   look   up   from   its   hiding   place   some   day   soon
t o   r e a c h   f o r   y o u r   f a c e   y o u r   e y e s

Questions Without Marks:

When I shove you:
you shove me back.
When I reach for
                    your
                    hand:
you   shove me again.

When I look at you:
you l o o k a w a y.
When
you l o o k a t m e:
I   l o o k a w a y.

When I see you in a room:
I turn the other way.
When I don't see you now:
I l o o k f o r y o u.

I l o o k f o r y o u.

First:

She   Refuses
To Admit My
Right   To
Breathe   Air
On This
Planet.

Then:
She   Agrees
To Allow My
Feet   Near
Her   Street.

Next
Then:
She   Answers
Her   Phone.

Now:
She   Listens.

First:

I
can
tell by your smile
and the way the sun
glints off your lower
b r a c e.

Real:

You
are
pulling me closer
with your eager
hands around my
w a i s t.

Kiss:

My
eyes
close   so tight
at the   perfect
moment of first
t a s t e.

This Hug,
This Kiss,
This Hand:

This
Life   Of
Love

       Of Five
       Fingers
       In Five
       Fingers
       In

This
Life   Of
Love.

This   Hand.
This   Hand.
This   Hand.

When This Boy Loves:

B i t e
Off My
Ginger-
    Bread
L e g s
And
I
Run To
You On
      My
Hands.

He
Really
Loves.

Not Every Sunset:

is the death
of the s u n.
There are tomorrows
that begin with brilliant light
blasting through my curtains,
to knock me out of bed.
Not every sunset
is even   the end
of the daily day.
There are nights
of flash and shine
that roll   without
                end
i n t o   morning:

y o u r
f a c e   in-
        can-
        des-
        scent
        in
        my
        r o o m.

Listen To The Voice In Your Head:

1. You will never be tall.
2. You will never be thin.
3. You will never have a chest (male or female variety)
                    that   will   cause   e x c i t e m e n t.
4. You will break   out
        with a h u g e
        pimple on your nose: the afternoon of TheBigGame,
                        the   evening   of TheBigDance.
5. You will break out.
6. You will break out.
7. You w i l l always
        break out.

8. No one will ever love you,
9. and the world will turn its great equatorial back on you,
10. and you will live in a swamp of defeat and self-pity,
11. and even your mother will stop making sandwiches;
12. and
    you will never be tall,
    you will never be thin.
13. You will break out
        f o r e v e r.
14. You w i l l always
            break out
        f o r e v e r.
15. You w i l l.
16. You will.
17. You.

Dear Self:

1.
Your
nose is an arrow
pointing   away
                far
                away
from
your   crooked
                eyes.
2.
Flies
rest on that top
                shelf
                of
                chin
below
your metal mouth.
3.
Your
satellite   dish
                ears
can pick up
K l i n g o n
                quiz
                show
r e r u n s.

At This Age,
This Time
Of Young Age:

I
walk
down
the
up escalator
backwards
      into
the west
      coast
sunrise
at
evening,
forward into
the east
      coast
sunset
at
morning,
      rocks
in my back
    pack.

Up Close And Personal(s):

1. I
   don't
   really
   need
   this
   bra.

2. I
   put
   my
   mother's
   make-
   up
   on
   this
   zit.

3. Sex
   is
   just
   a
   four-
   letter
   word.

He: **:ehS**

There   erehT
is   si
hair   riah
on   no
my   ym
upper   reppu
lip.   .pil

Now:

This
time

from
trolls
to
tampax

says
it
all.

Bump   Stick
      er   er:

Cute   Cool
ness   ness
kills.   thrills.

Skin Games #1:

My
cheeks
are
covered
with
a
fine
red
rash
that
lights
up
bright
as
Christmas
when
you
pass
me
down
the
hall.
My
arms
are
always
red
and
tree
branch
thin;
and
my
legs:
legs
as
thin
and
red
as
my
arms.
But
my
eyes
are
mirrors
for
your
fine
brown
face,
and
you
always
smile.

Skin Games #2:

Your then which smile
permanent sit planet and
tan at you lean
this our come your
winter table from, dark
looks tomorrow then curls
so morning, move into
great then next my
against transfer door. nose,
white to Just then
snow. my smile simply
Ski home and move
with room, move next
me then next door
this tell door. right
afternoon, me Please now.

Here In Our City:

b i r d s   s i n g.
City   roaches   are   as   big   as   country   mice:
our   mice   as   fat   as   long-tail   water   rats.
City   rats   are   as   round   as   well-fed   cats:
our   cats   as   great   as   Afghan   Hounds   under
the park trees across from school.

And in those trees   as   our   city   birds   sing:
their wings spread from   limb to limb, covering
highest branches   with   fine   feathered b i r d
b e l l i e s. Long   feet   drag   the   ground.
The morning sky darkens   when they rise to fly.
Their city songs break ear drums and curl toes.

On my way to school   this morning   I see   truck
drivers delivering and dumping   loads   of   seed
on
to the park fields. They wear   steel   earmuffs
as   thick   as   frying   pans   tied a r o u n d
their heads   with rubber scarves.   We shut the
windows of our
room
before first class.

Stepping Off The Morning School Bus:

my umbrella gets caught in a great   gust of wind
a n d   t u r n s   i n s i d e   o u t
just in time to catch my   carefully coifed curls
in a tropical downpour   here   in the great northwest.
I step into the high school building
with curtains of long dripping hair
hanging down from my equally soaked, flat-topped head.

O f   c o u r s e :
here comes Steel String Sting-like Stanley,
AKA Stanley Hochmeyer, lead guitar and definitive
heart throb of our local rock band, Pubic Sound.
I want to melt into a wicked witch puddle on the
hallway floor. I want to be blown away by
a sudden gust of assistant principal hot
air. I want to run in fast forward motion
                              t o   f i r s t   c l a s s .

But I stand frozen, from top of flat head
to bottom of ugly g r e e n   b o o t s ,
w h i l e   S t a n l e y   A i r   D a n c e s past:
h i s   s p a r k l i n g   t e e t h   j u s t inches
from my   obviously invisible   wet and red face.

Your Sweet Words:

fill   my   head
and   heart
and stomach.
Your
complimentary
   observations
inflate   this
large   tire
around   this
boyish   middle.
Acne pops
pop out
pop up
pictures
on   my
flushed cheeks
each time you
roll my   name
around your mouth
and   slide   it   out
in   my   direction.
I need to   immunize early
with a   preventive medicine:
with immediate   injections
of   intellectual   in su lin.
One   kiss   at   the   library
will cure
or   kill.

Summer Session:

Just when you thought
it was safe to go back
i n t o the l o v e l y
                    c o o l
                  water
a
giant gull s w o o p s
                    d o w n
and grabs
your feeble arms
in its beak   and   flies
                              you
to Mrs. Gruber's
early   morning
every   morning
m a t h e m a t i c s
m i s f o r t u n e
                    until
                  August.

I Wear This Shirt:

outside my pants
to hide this unhealthy-
looking pot popping my
buckle out into the space
between my belly and any approaching
                                    girl.
I need to do gymnastics
to be near the cheer-
leaders after
school.

Winter is the best:
heavy coats and jackets
cover the belly of this
soft
body
boy.

This Game Is Never Called:

1.
We play on,
slogging through
softening mud,
as the rain comes
down
harder
this late afternoon.

2.
My
cleats
stick
as I turn to run,
and I fall to my knees
with the brown splash
of a whale in blue shorts.

3.
When he pulls me up
by my elbow
and helps me
off the field,
there is an almost
too rough tug
to his arm.

4.
But
I think
his
eyes
show
care
and

5.
c l o s e
c o n c e r n.

Real World News Flash:

You
are a mediocre
player sitting on
the bench of an intra-
mural team during a losing
season in front of empty gym bleachers.

Standing Very Still:

with a cool breeze
        b l o w i n g,
I still   can   feel
the   trickle   of
        s w e a t
    d r i p p i n g
         d o w n
from u n d er arms;
down   my   sides
as
I simply   stand
          and
         watch
you
  simply   walk
        down
the steps
of   the
bleachers.

Under The Stands:

                              while
                    the   bands
are
marching,
and
the drum major is dancing
down the field   with his
h i g h   k i c k i n g   legs
and   arching-backwards back,
they
shoot
smack
at
half
time.

Chemistry Lesson After Class:

Angel Dust. Zombie Dust. PCP. Elephant Tranquilizer.
Busy Bee: Added To Marijuana Cigarettes.
Available At Your Local Connection. Dan
White Crystal Powder.   ger
A n g e l   D u s t.   ous.
                                                Dan
                                                ger
                                                ous.
                                                Dan
                                                ger
                                                ous.

This Car Always Stops:

at the Hamburger Heaven parking lot,
and
one guy stays at the w h e e l
with the motor r u n n i n g,
while the other guy
                    s h o w s
us
an attaché case
    full of reds
    and   greens
    and   nickel
    b   a   g   s.

He says he is going from town to town
along our Old Route 40 h i g h w a y
until he is s o l d
                o u t.
And he always m a k e s
it home b e f o r e the
II o'c l o c k n e ws.

Equal Opportunity Employment:

The cops have busted
the
big time dope dealer
behind the wheel   of
                    his
Continental car.
He
stopped for a red
light
late at
night
while making rounds.
The
next day
there was a new man
behind the wheel and
she was a woman.
But
the same old car keeps
rolling up and down our
    neighborhood streets.

**Did
You
Hear:**

That Ken And Barbie Got Busted
For Doing Some Heavy Colombian
Green In Their Funtime Kamper?

Captain America Was The Connection.
Robin Was The Runner. Batman Cried.
The Joker Lied As Usual.
Superman Sang A Song.

O Mighty Isis.
O Athena.
O Shazzams
        And
    Shazzam-
        Nots Of This Play Time Play Ground:
    Give Us The Power To Play It Straight.
Did
You
Hear: We Look In The Mirror For Our New Heroes.

Just Say No:

to
unborn
t w i n k i e s
t w i n k l ing
from
plastic
placenta
packages.
Period.

(And when his addiction grew too strong
to control, he would buy by the box; and
behind the super market, behind the giant
dumpsters, snort them (unwrapped) up
                                              his
                                           pain-
                                           fully
distended nostrils; until the l e t h a l
combo of yellow cake, white s u g a r and
g r e a s e would clog those   breathing
                                        passages,
clear up to his stupifying brain.)
And he would slide down to sit in a daze
u n t i l   t h e   g a r b a g e   t r u c
                                                k
                                                .

                                                .

                                                .

Almost Ready:

I as
am this
going cool
to and
her in-
birth- control
day young
party dude:

as	as	as	as
soon	soon	soon	soon
as	as	as	as
I	I	I	I
find	find	find	find
my	my	my	my
new	hip	deep	right
shirt,	shoes,	voice,	mask.

Bopping For Chips:

First   we find the biggest bowl:
some   industrial   chilli pot, or
some stew kettle, or t u r   key
roasting pan.   Then we rip open
a dozen bags of   hand-cut   Ohio
deep-fried   thick   and   rippled
h e a v y   s a l t e d
p   o   t   a   t   o   chips.

When you miss the answer to the trivia question,
when you miss the question about a n y t h i n g
unimportant in   your   young life, you h a v e
                              to d u n k
                              y o u r
                              f a c e
                              d e e p

into the bowl of chips,
and stuff your mouth
and rise up chewing,
(not spitting)   chips.
            Chips must fall from behind ears:
            salt on your nose and lashes.

Warning: Corn chips will cut your cheekbones
          to shreds.   Cheese noodles   will
          clog   your   nostrils   dangerously.
          Always stay   away   from apples.
            Stay   away   from apples.
            Stay   away.   Apples.
                              Apples.
                              Apples.

Freeze Frame:

My
right
pinkie
is
in
my
left
nostril
digging
for
gold
when
you
walk
by.

Singing To Japanese Fishermen:

The whales are sounding
down the California c o a s t,
                            o
                              o
              and clouds of n o t e s
                            o
                              o
                    f o l l o w
                            o
                              o
              their f l o a t i n g bulks
                            o
                              o
              to M e x i c o.

                            O
                              o
                    You are conducting
                    this symphony with
                    bloody dolphin
                                    f i n s
from   your   invincible   ships:
invisible   in   the   blue   air
              of   the   Pacific.
You   hold   your   sharpened
                    harpoons
for
the sad red end
of this s o n g.

On The Way To His Funeral:

I close my eyes
in the back seat
of the black limo
moving slowly down
our empty street.
I dream:
I am going to school
in hard hat and flak
jacket. I walk through
the metal detector only
to enter into empty halls
and open echo classrooms.
But
our
dead
bodies
are
stacked
high,
covering the gym floor.
M y b l a c k s h o e s
s l i d e i n b l o o d .

On the way to his funeral
I open my eyes
in the back seat
of the black limo
moving slowly down
our empty street.

Skin Games #3:

They
raise
the
safety
numbers
so
high
on
sun-
tan
bottles,
for
their
sales,
you
might
as
well

rub
charcoal
on
your
cheeks.
The
most
un-
cool
cancer
rays
keep
zapping
through
the
o-
zone
holes:

our
legacy
to
babies
on
the
beach.
Beyond
the
mel-
a-
nine
your
mom/
pop
gene
pool
re-

produced:
floats
jazz
and
blues.
Spread
hip
hop
on
your
ears
for
safest
tanning
of
the
inner
skin.

Skin Games #4:

Your Your We
father mother should
still still be
hustles holds brothers.
to her We
make job, should
enough just be
to like arm
pay my in
the mom. arm,
bills And and
each you always
month, do together
even most in
with dinners this
his in tough
straight an and
blond empty green
hair. house. world.

I Ride In The Back:

while my older sister   drives up front, of course,
with Hunk Man Harry High School Heat Treat.
Smoke rises from the approximate place in space
where his "very forward" Big Brown Eyes   meet
her lashing lashes, her dashing   glancing glances:
from road traffic to his drooling mouth, and back
to the corner stop sign of the serious real world.

She acts as if it had been
installed   only   a   second
before by extraterrestrial
traffic   safety   engineers.
Her brakes   squeal   louder
than her mouth says sorry,
and I know we need to talk
i f w e   e v e r get home.

You Never Really Listen To Me:

Me,
I see it simple.
My broken toe: oh yes.
But
momma, you translate me
from   EnglishintoEnglish
and toe turns into heart:
       oh broken-hearted-baby-daughter-girl,
       you are s t i l l t o o y o u n g
       to   feel   that   way.

Momma,
why don't you try and keep me from feeling
                 rain drops on my face?
Why don't you try and keep me from feeling
          s u m m e r   s u n?
Momma,
why do you still try?
You know you can't keep me from feeling.
You   really   can't keep me from feeling.
You   really   can't keep me
          s t i l l t o o y o u n g.
Beyond
the broken toe and homework grades,
you m u s t really listen to me.

Grounded:

Too   old
a   n   d
too   fast
to   be hit,
I   can   usually
be   found   in
my   dark room
up   against a
c o l d   wall:
        A
        C
        D
        C
blasting into
right
    and
left
e a r phones:
right
    and
wrong.

Walking Along The Edge
Of The Back Yard:

Our
old
sand
box
full   of years   of leaves
and   broken   branches
and   especially cat scat,
is
almost buried under the
          osage orange hedge,
but
still
here.
One
yellow caterpillar earth-
mover lies on its side
                    beside
my last favorite red
dump truck full of
rainwater   and rust.
I
will
always
m a k e that
motor sound
          with
              my
          mouth.

The Usual Sunday Evening:

Nine P.M.
and
the last whole wheat pizza order
to be filled tonight   has been filled tonight.
So we close the doors and I can begin to mop
the floors. The salad bar is covered. I ate
                                the
last of the bean sprouts in my pita bread
sandwich. We are out of soy cheese until
tomorrow afternoon's delivery truck. The
                         streets
of my town are as empty
as my Sunday evening
head. Only the single
traffic light changes
on electronic program:
green to red to green. I supply the go slow
                    y e l l o w   caution:
                    there is home w o r k
                    waiting under the pile
                    of dirty sweats   on
                                  my
                          desk.

The usual Sunday evening.

Got Ta   Got Ta   Got Ta   Got Ta:

                              have your
                              b u r n i n
                              b u r n i n
                              b u r n i n
                                   love.

Got ta
have
your
sweet potato,
apple pie,
mandarin orange,
brown-sugar-on-oatmeal-
in-the-cold-winter-mornings-
sandwich-in-the-lunch-bag-and-
sun-shining-on-snow-drifts-kind
                              of
                    l o v e.

Got
    ta
got
    ta
got
    ta
got
got
got.

I Had This Dream Last Night:

They threw me out of the dance
because
the pimple on the end of my nose
was
so big and bright
it
lit up the whole gym,
especially during the slow songs.
And
you stood and laughed
at
me
until t h e captain
of
the
f o o t b a l l
team
walked over and wiped the drool
from the corner of your mouth.
Then you had to walk arminarm:
Garth and Whitney into the dark.
They threw me out of the dance
and
they slammed s h u t the door.

All The Right Things
Turn Out Wrong
Song:

This morning   in my bed,
the clouds   were so low
I bumped   my head   when
                              I sat up.
There
was   grey   cloud   in my
ears, and   the pants   on
my chair   were   covered
with tears.   And
                              t h e
bed was getting wet.
                              And
                                    it
                              was   raining in my mouth.
Oh,
I'm so sad
It's raining
in my mouth. I taste it.
Oh,
I'm so sad
It's raining
up my nose. I smell it.
Oh,
I'm so sad
It's raining
in my eyes. I cry it.

This Love Song Singing Just To You:

Surround me like the sky
          when I take wing.
We are together: a   duet
                    of angels. We rise over the ocean
                              and   into   the   blue
                                                      of
                                                    eyes.

You   are   a   time   traveler
living within your limitless
                imagination.
You
are apparition   suddenly   within human condition.

Surround me like the sky
          when I take wing.
I w a n t to look at you
the   w a y I first saw you.
I am beyond understanding.
Stay
slowly
f o r t h i s singing of the song.

There Is Only One Music:

Beyond
s k i n and age,
language, b e a t,
melodic m o v e
and the   great
        ancestral
            g r o o v e
of
e a c h people in
all   geographies
and   generations:
there is only one   music.
Really,
there is only one   song.

I love you. Do you love me? You must love me.
Can we get together and be in love? Let's sing.
Let's dance. Let's sing and dance and party with
each other into the long years of cereal boxes.
If we cannot live forever, can we live together?
Can we sing this song of love into dead streets?
Can we sing this song of life into the cardboard
shelter boxes of the hungry? Will hate triumph?
I love you. Do you love me? You must love me.
Can we get together and be in love? Let's sing.
Remember:
there is only one   music.
Really,
there is only one   song.

slow dance heart break blues:

asking
      finally   rejecting   asking   rejecting askingasking
there has to be the asking and the rejecting and the yes
finally dance and the holding of hands the laughing and
the very awkward silences silences in the touching the
fingers in the touching of fingertips is the power that
double amps the band juice from hand to hand jamming us
into that place past wonder past cool
needing
      again to know who will kiss who good night who
will walk together after the dance down the hall to the
waiting car and who will touch and what will not happen
what is like what is love what is lust and what
good bye becomes hello becomes hello and alwayshello
                                     and

will the sun for real rise up tomorrow
and
will we live forever
and
will we do some good
      for some people while we are on
      t h i s   true   b l u e   p l a n e t
      for this crooked   eye wink of time
and
will I ever learn to love me f i r s t
will I ever learn to love you as strong
will I ever wear the bottoms of my black
      jeans rolled and shave one side of
      my head and have the p e a c e sign
      carved into the short hairs on the
      other side while my top knot of
      rasta braids w a v e s in advanced
      algebra class all the way to MIT
dancing
      s l o w within your smile m y
      answers shoot out of your eyes
sending
 ending

Arnold Adoff

was born in New York City on the hot Sunday afternoon of July 16, 1935. He grew up in The Bronx, and as a young man spent countless hours in Greenwich Village, the Museum of Modern Art, and Birdland. An alumnus of the City College of New York, he studied American Intellectual History at Columbia University.

Arnold claims three fathers: Aaron Jacob Adoff; Charles Mingus, the extraordinary jazz bassist and composer; and José Garcia Villa, poet and teacher. Since 1968, he has published thirty-three books, including anthologies, works of "poet's prose," and poetry. He writes for children, young adults, and their older allies of all ages. Some of his books include *All the Colors of the Race, Chocolate Dreams, Sports Pages, Eats, Flamboyan,* and *Street Music.* His work has received many awards and honors over the years, including the NCTE Poetry Award.

Arnold travels, lectures, teaches, and reads aloud with style and passion. He is married to the celebrated American novelist, Virginia Hamilton. They have two grown children: Leigh Hamilton, an operatic soprano, and Jaime Levi, a rock singer and songwriter.